The kangaroo lives only in Australia.

The kangaroo has a long, thick tail. It can rest on its tail while standing.

Mother kangaroos have a pouch in front of their stomach. When a baby kangaroo is born, it gets in the pouch and stays there for about 6 months.

Using its large, strong back feet, a kangaroo can jump about 10 feet high and 30 feet in distance!

Kangaroos spend hot days resting in the
shade. They go out only at night to
eat and drink.

Kangaroos eat the short, fresh grass that grows in the meadows.

The kangaroo is a shy animal.

Kangaroos like to be neat and clean. They use their claws like a comb.

When it doesn't rain for a while, kangaroos find water by digging in the ground.

A kangaroo has long ears that can
move together or one at a time
in the direction of sound.